# Small Game Hunting

By Christopher L. Eger

ELDORADO INK

**Eldorado Ink**
PO Box 100097
Pittsburgh, PA 15233
www.eldoradoink.com

Produced by OTTN Publishing, Stockton, New Jersey

CPSIA compliance information: Batch#RGO2014-1.
For further information, contact Eldorado Ink at info@eldoradoink.com.

First printing

1  3  5  7  9  8  6  4  2

Library of Congress Cataloging-in-Publication Data

Eger, Christopher L., author.
  Small game hunting / Christopher L. Eger.
      pages cm. — (Responsible gun ownership)
  Audience: 9 to 12.
  Includes bibliographical references and index.
      ISBN 978-1-61900-052-0 (hc)
      ISBN 978-1-61900-058-2 (trade)
      ISBN 978-1-61900-064-3 (ebook)
  1. Small game hunting.  I. Title.
  SK340.E34 2014
  799.2'5—dc23

                                          2014000388

*For information about custom editions, special sales, or premiums,
please contact our special sales department at info@eldoradoink.com.*

# Table of Contents

1. Just What Is Small Game Hunting?............5
2. Hunting Safety .........................................9
3. Tools of the Trade ....................................15
4. Tips and Tricks .......................................27
5. Hunting Feathered Game........................33
6. Hunting Furred Game ............................45
7. After the Hunt........................................51

Glossary......................................................56
Further Reading .........................................59
Internet Resources .....................................60
Index ..........................................................62
About the Author/Photo Credits.................64

*Chapter 1*

# Just What Is Small Game Hunting?

**H**unting can be one of the most enjoyable experiences that you can have in the woods of North America. This most human of undertakings dates back to prehistoric times. The first cave dwellers spent a large part of their lives in the pursuit of wild game. Over time, humans have moved from the caves, discovered electricity, and even landed on the moon—yet we continue to hunt.

Hunting has evolved over the centuries, just as humans did. At one time, humans hunted to feed themselves and their families. Today, people can find all the food they need with a visit to their local supermarket. However, many people still enjoy the challenge of hunting, whether it is stalking larger animals like deer, elk, and turkey, or hunting smaller game.

The small game hunter may find himself or herself stalking or flushing out a variety of animals—anything from upland birds like quail and doves to numerous four-legged creatures smaller than a deer, from squirrels to wild hogs. The variety of small game animals presents a wide range of challenges to the hunter. For instance, it takes different skills and techniques to wait patiently for a covey of quail than it does to search at night for raccoons. It's this variety that helps keep small game hunting so popular.

## AN INTRODUCTION TO HUNTING

Often, young people begin their education as hunters and woodsmen by tracking and hunting small game. The lessons that they learn while hunting for squirrels, rabbits, and other abundant woodland creatures provide a foundation of skills that can be used on future expeditions against larger or more challenging game.

Remember, for many people hunting is a sport just like softball, swimming, or gymnastics. In any sport, participants must start with the basics, practice a lot to develop their skills, and keep things simple. As your skills develop, you get better and can move on to bigger challenges. And unlike most team sports, hunting is a sport that you can enjoy at any age.

Small game hunting can also be the gateway to a whole set of other outdoor activities, like hiking, camping, orienteering, and geocaching. Once you have mastered your hunting skills, you can share with others what you have learned.

## CONSERVATION

Every hunter is a conservationist. Webster's Dictionary defines the word as, "someone who works to protect animals, plants, and natural resources or to prevent the loss or waste of natural resources." Hunters are champions of the environment and are the biggest leaders in its preservation. The only thing a good hunter leaves behind in the field is his footprints. Responsible hunters take only the game they can use and spare the rest.

Under a law known as the Pittman-Robertson Act that was adopted in 1937, the federal government started to maintain birds and mammals in their natural habitat. This preservation is what has led to the huge series of wildlife refuges across the country. The Pittman-Robertson Act is funded by taxes on guns and ammunition. This means that every rifle, shotgun, ammunition cartridge, or shell sold in

*The term "small game" covers a wide range of animals. In general, it refers to birds smaller than a wild turkey and four-legged animals smaller than a deer. Rabbits, ducks, and pheasants are among the most popular small game.*

the country for the past 75 + years, contributes money toward preserving our environmental resources for future generations to enjoy.

To some people it is hard to understand how hunters, who kill wild animals, are protecting the environment. However, by harvesting a certain number of animals each season, hunters help keep the natural population of those animals at a level that can be supported by their habitat. Years ago, natural predators such as wolves, bears, and cougars performed this function. However, as the number of natural predators has dwindled, the populations of small woodland creatures such as squirrels, doves, and rabbits have risen. Without proper management, the total population of these animals would reach a level where they exhaust their supply of food, leading to starvation and suffering. This is where hunters come in.

The federal government has long conducted an extensive survey of migratory birds. These birds, which include doves, woodcocks, rails and snipe, roam from state to state. To get a count of just how many of these birds there are, the government uses the Migratory Bird Harvest Information Program (HIP). The information that HIP gets comes directly from paperwork filled out by small game hunters. From that raw data, conservation efforts can be adjusted to keep animal populations at ideal numbers for the environment.

Therefore, the small game hunters of today are a vital part of keeping the ecosystem on the right course.

*Chapter 2*

# Hunting Safety

E very sport relies on a set of safety rules to make sure that participants have a good time without getting hurt. Hunting is no exception to this. Because firearms are involved, careful adherence to safety rules is absolutely necessary. Hunting can be both fun and safe, as long as everyone keeps these tips in mind at all times. Remember, if you don't take the woods seriously, you shouldn't be in them.

## GUN SAFETY

Before 1937, firearms used to be one of the leading causes of accidents while hunting. Since then, through increased hunter's education, hunting has become one of the safest sports in the country. In fact, according to the National Shooting Sports Foundation, you are 25 times more likely to be injured cheerleading, and 105 times more likely to be hurt playing football, than you are to be injured while hunting. This is not because firearms themselves are safer, but because hunters are better educated about safety and proper firearm handling procedures. Firearms safety begins with observing the following four critical rules:

1. ALWAYS POINT THE GUN BARREL IN A SAFE DIRECTION. A safe direction is one in which an accidental discharge will not cause injury to yourself or to another person. You should never point a rifle or shotgun at another person, unless you intend to shoot that person in self-defense. Even if your rifle or shotgun is unloaded, be aware of the direction it is pointed. This is the most important rule of firearm safety. It is particularly important to observe this First Commandment any time you load or unload your weapon.

2. TREAT ALL GUNS AS IF THEY ARE LOADED. The most avoidable firearms-related accidents are the ones in which people are injured or killed by a gun the handler just "knew" was unloaded. If you always treat every gun as if it is loaded—even when you have checked and know that the gun is not loaded—it is almost impossible to have a negligent discharge. Proper muzzle discipline makes this possible.

3. KEEP YOUR FINGER OFF THE TRIGGER UNTIL READY TO FIRE. While it is remotely possible that a gun could go off for no rea-

*Always unload your firearm when walking through areas where the footing may be poor, such as over loose rock or on steep hillsides, or when crossing obstacles such as fences, streams, or ditches.*

*Never fire your rifle at a target that is "sky-lined," such as one standing or moving at the top of a hill. If you miss your target, your bullet might injure a person that you can't see.*

son, typically a gun won't fire unless the trigger is pulled. Therefore, if you make sure that your finger is outside of your gun's trigger guard until you are lined up on your target, the odds of it going off accidentally are slim. This is especially important when you're walking through the woods carrying a rifle or shotgun. If you stumble and fall with your finger on the trigger, you may accidentally pull it, adding a stray round to your problems.

4. BE SURE OF YOUR TARGET, AND WHAT IS BEYOND IT. If you think that you are shooting at a dove or rabbit, but are not 100 percent certain, then don't shoot. The rattle of bushes or movement in the distance is not something to shoot at blindly. It could very well be another hunter making that noise.

Moreover, be aware of what is beyond where you are shooting. Even small caliber bullets such as .22LR rimfires can travel for a mile or more. If you are shooting in a field and a house, car, and/or road are in sight, chances are all of the above will be in within range of your firearm.

## OTHER GUN SAFETY RULES

While you need to drill the four rules above into your head, there are other important safety practices to keep in mind. These include keeping your firearms unloaded when not in use, never climbing a fence or tree with a loaded firearm, and never leaning a loaded gun against a tree or stump. These rules will help avoid accidents.

If you ever drop your rifle or shotgun in the woods, first unload it and then check the barrel to make sure it is not clogged with mud, rocks, or dirt. Firing a gun with a clogged barrel—even one that is partly clogged—can result in an explosion that will destroy your gun and possibly injure you badly.

Bullets are not the magic projectiles depicted in Hollywood movies. They will ricochet if fired at hard, flat surfaces—including rocks, cement, metal, and even calm bodies of water. Always be aware of that danger when taking aim at a target.

Eye and ear protection should be used not only on the shooting range but in the field as well. It only takes one gunshot to damage your hearing, or one piece of debris to damage your sight forever. Always wear shooting glasses and either earplugs or earmuffs.

Finally, alcohol and drugs have no place when firearms are present. Stay away from these before or during hunting and make sure that those with you do so as well.

## Be Seen

Remember that part above about being sure of your target? Well, when you're in the woods, being a target is the last thing you want. Wearing a "hunter orange" safety vest and hat can help make you visible in the woods to other hunters. Many states have requirements for what color, and how much of that color (in square inches of coverage), have to be worn when hunting, so be sure to check the requirements for your area before heading into the woods.

Although safety colors are not required in all states, it is a good idea to wear them any time you are small game hunting. A recent study by the New York Department of Environmental Conservation found that hunters not wearing orange were seven times more likely to be shot accidentally.

Don't worry that the bright orange color will scare away your game. Studies have shown that many animals, including deer and most small game, have trouble distinguishing orange from red and green. This means that they are essentially color-blind when it comes to hunter orange. However, turkeys as well as small game birds like waterfowl and doves have more sensitive eyesight. Duck hunters should wear blaze orange when walking to and from their hunting blind, but wear camouflage while waiting for a target to appear.

One more pointer on colors in the woods—during deer season, avoid wearing brown or tan colors when hunting. The last thing you want to be is a flash of brown between the trees when the woods are filled with armed men looking for deer.

## THE HUNTING PLAN

Before you go into the woods, always leave a hunting plan behind. This can be a simple note that you give to someone you trust. Write down when and where you are going and when you expect to be back. Do not just tell someone; give that person a written note. This way if something happens to you they can pass on the information. Instruct the person with the note to call the local sheriff or wildlife office if they haven't heard from you by a certain time.

If you will be hunting on public land, it's a good idea to check in with the local game warden or ranger beforehand. Another good idea is to leave an extra copy of your hunting plan in your car, just in case. Hopefully you will never have a problem, but you should never go into the woods without leaving your hunting plan behind, just in case.

If possible, avoid hunting alone. If an accident occurs, having another person nearby can be the difference between life and death. Having a hunting buddy can add more to the experience than just an extra measure of safety. Some of the best times in the woods can come from spending the day hunting with a friend, even if you don't get a single thing.

## Lost and Found

Even the most experienced woodsman can get lost. This can happen faster than you realize. Make two wrong turns on a trail and you can find yourself confused and alone in the woods. The first thing to do if you find yourself in this situation is to remain calm. The second thing is to remember the first.

As the old U.S. Forestry Service advice says, "Use your head, not your legs." Do not simply start wandering around, as this can result in making you even more lost. Stop and think about how you got to this point before trying to retrace your steps. This is when a cellphone or mobile GPS device can prove its worth. Another lightweight item that can help when lost is a whistle. It's always easier to blow a whistle repeatedly then it is to yell for help.

If you must move, look for trails, roads, or streams; once you find one, follow it. The likelihood of them leading to civilization is much higher than wandering around aimlessly. In addition, these routes will probably be the ones on which you will be more likely bump into other hunters.

Remember the "Survival Rule of Threes" when having to survive in the wild. You can survive for three minutes without air, three hours without shelter, three days without water, and three weeks without food. While many hunters go into the woods with food and water, and air is free, they often forget the more important challenge of shelter.

Once night starts to fall, stop and settle in. Do not try to move around in the dark. Try to find or build shelter to stay warm. A small emergency thermal blanket can come in handy if you become lost. These blankets, made from Mylar insulating material, are inexpensive (typically under $10), don't weigh much, and can fit in a back pocket. They do a good job of reflecting your body heat back to you, keeping you warm. Remember, most hunting takes place during fall or winter months, and spending a night alone and cold is no fun.

If you follow the safety rules and simple tips outlined in this chapter, small game hunting should be a safe and enjoyable activity.

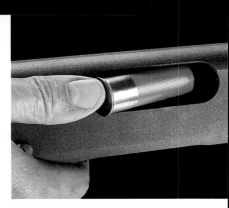

## Chapter 3

# Tools of the Trade

Small game hunters typically are looking to harvest animals that weigh less than 40 pounds. This includes varmints like chipmunks, skunk, and raccoon, as well as small predators like coyote and bobcat. Other furred game like rabbit and squirrel are high on the list of popular targets as well. All of these animals can be taken reliably with a rifle.

Small caliber rifles, such as those chambered for the .22LR rimfire ammunition cartridge, are ideal for taking small game. They are simple to use, highly accurate, and very affordable, with used models that are in good condition selling for around $100. The .22LR ammunition is also inexpensive—it is by far the most popular ammunition in the world.

A downside to the .22LR cartridge is that its range is somewhat limited; beyond about 150 yards (137 m), the bullet may not have enough accuracy or power to guarantee a kill. Remember, responsible hunters are conservationists—you need to respect the animals that you hunt, and to reflect that respect you must make every effort to harvest animals cleanly,

*The .22LR rimfire cartridge is popular among small-game hunters because it is inexpensive to shoot but powerful enough to bring down small animals at a range of less than 100 yards (91 m). Bullets with a hollow point (right) will expand, or mushroom when they hit the target, causing greater damage.*

not leave them wounded to wander away to suffer and die in the woods. So when hunting with a rifle chambered for .22LR ammunition, your ideal shot will come at a range of 50 to 100 yards (46 to 91 m).

If you want to hunt varmints or small game at a greater distance, you can expand your range to about 250 yards (229 m) by using rifles chambered for the more powerful .22WMR and .17 HMR rounds. These are known as "magnum" rounds because the bullet is heavier than a .22LR bullet, and the brass case is longer to allow more grains of propellant. This allows for higher muzzle velocity and a more powerful impact.

Centerfire rifles are typically more powerful than rimfire rifles, but be careful when choosing one for small game hunting, as you can easily go into overkill. For instance, you would not want to use a rifle chambered in .30-06 to hunt rabbits. If you hit one, there would not be enough rabbit left to be worthwhile. Some states limit the caliber of centerfire rifles that can be used during small game seasons; this is meant to help reduce deer poaching.

Good centerfire rifle choices for the small game hunter include models chambered for the .22 Hornet and .218 Bee cartridges. For coyote-sized animals, rifles chambered for .223 Remington, .22-250 Remington, and .25-06 Remington are popular. However, these are powerful, high-velocity rounds that can't be used to hunt lighter game.

### WHAT KIND OF RIFLE?

Once you figure out what caliber, now you have to select your rifle. There are many different types as well as different makers. Besides that, each maker sells or used to sell a number of different models of rifle.

The action is a mechanism that moves a cartridge into a rifle's chamber so it can be fired. Some rifles load only one ammunition cartridge at a time. These sometimes have a hinge action, which breaks open with the press of a level. Since the design is so simple, there are few parts to break or jam, making this sort of rifle very reliable. Manufacturers like H&R and Rossi have made guns of this type for years.

Other rifles can hold multiple ammunition cartridges, often in a magazine under the barrel or inside the stock. In this sort of rifle, working the action removes the spent shell casing and introduces a fresh cartridge. These rifles come in bolt-action, lever-action, and semi-automatic.

Bolt-action rifles have been around for over a century. These feed a round into the chamber by using a turning bolt that the hunter cycles by hand. They can either be single-shot or hold several rounds in a magazine built into the gun. Since there are more moving parts, these guns require more training and experience to operate than the hinge-break guns above. Almost every gun maker in the country that makes rifles markets bolt-action designs including Winchester, Remington, Ruger, and Savage.

Lever action guns are like bolt-actions in that they move a round of ammunition in and out of the chamber with the user moving part of the gun by hand. Instead of a bolt, these rifles have a lever under and around the trigger. These guns are like the 'cowboy guns' of the old western movies. Henry, Marlin, and others sell popular models.

Finally, semi-automatic rifles load and unload ammunition without the user having to do anything but pull the trigger. Since there is no bolt or lever to move by hand after each shot, all the user has to do is pull the trigger again and the rifle will fire. These guns can be very

*Single-shot bolt-action .22 rifles like this one are ideal for young hunters.*

useful to the small game hunter as they allow faster follow-up shots if the first shot misses the target. Like bolt-action rifles, almost every maker markets these guns.

## SHOTGUNS

Possibly even more than rifles, shotguns are the small game hunter's best friend. This is because these guns are much more versatile than a rifle. For example, a .22LR bolt-action rifle is just the thing for clearing an apple orchard of rabbits, but what can it do in that same orchard against game birds like dove and quail? Or what about hunting a larger animal, like a coyote?

Now take a 20-gauge shotgun in that same circumstance. Shotguns take a wide variety of different shells. These shells vary in the amount of "shot" they carry. For instance, a 20-gauge shotgun shell can hold either 585 pellets of Number 9 shot, which is ideal for small birds, or 21 pellets of Number 4 buck, which would work like magic on a fox. And if you want to go after larger game, you can always load 00 or 000 buckshot or a slug into that same 20-gauge and head into the woods. A rifle does not have this sort of versatility.

Shotguns do have limitations, though. They are not extremely accurate. This is because of the nature of their shells and the fact that most shotguns do not have very good sights. Taking a headshot on a chipmunk with a 12-gauge is like threading a needle with a rope. It just isn't going to happen.

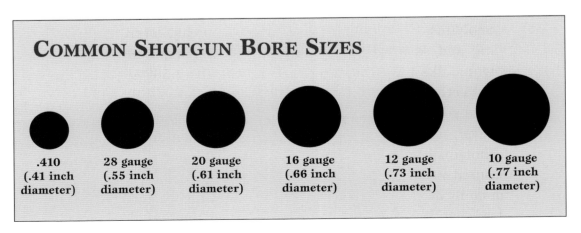

### COMMON SHOTGUN BORE SIZES

| .410 (.41 inch diameter) | 28 gauge (.55 inch diameter) | 20 gauge (.61 inch diameter) | 16 gauge (.66 inch diameter) | 12 gauge (.73 inch diameter) | 10 gauge (.77 inch diameter) |

*Traditionally, shot is made of lead. However, in the United States it is no longer legal to use lead shot when hunting waterfowl, because game birds eat shot from the bottoms of lakes and waterways, then die from lead poisoning. In some federal game lands, lead shot is prohibited for upland bird hunting as well. Today, non-toxic shot is made from steel, tungsten, or bismuth. These materials are less dense than lead and tend to fly differently, so smart hunters practice with the same ammunition that they intend to use in the field.*

The shotgun makes up for this lack of accuracy by sending large amounts of lead downrange. Remember that figure above of 585 Number 9 shot in a 20-gauge shotgun shell? That translates into hundreds of .079-inch wide lead pellets heading towards your target at the same time. This "spread" of shot grows at a rate of about one inch every three feet. Therefore, those hundreds of pellets will be in a cloud about the size of a basketball by the time it is 10 yards (9 m) from you. With that in mind, you can see the benefits of a shotgun against small targets at relatively close ranges. If your target is 50 yards (46 m) or more away, the shot pattern will likely be too big to ensure good hits.

Shotguns, like rifles, are sold in hinge-break, lever-action, bolt-action, and semi-automatic. There are also pumps, or slide-action shotguns, like the Remington 870 and Mossberg 500 series that are very effective.

Like rifles, shotguns are classified by the diameter of their bore. However, rather than using a caliber measurement like a rifle, nearly all shotgun bores are measured in gauge. (One type of shotgun is measured in caliber—the .410, which is the smallest shotgun bore commonly available.) Gauge is determined by the weight of a solid ball of lead that fits inside the shotgun bore. A ball that weighs one-twelfth of a pound fits into a 12-gauge shotgun, for example, while a smaller ball that weighs one-twentieth of a pound fits in a 20-gauge shotgun. The lower the gauge, the larger the shotgun's bore. The most popular shotguns are 12 or 20 gauge. Other common shotgun gauges are 10, 16, or 28 gauge.

## HANDGUNS

Like rifles, handguns have a place in hunting small game. Many states allow the use of .22 caliber pistols and revolvers for this type of hunting. Before heading to the woods with your handgun, be sure of your local laws.

Due to the shorter sight radius on handguns, hitting small targets with one can be very challenging. With this in mind, hunting small game with a handgun is not for the newcomer. You should be able to hit a target the size of a walnut repeatedly with your pistol before heading to the woods. Long barreled pistols such as the Ruger MkIII, Beretta Neo, and revolvers such as the Ruger Single Six and Smith and Wesson K-22 can all work nicely for small game if the hunter puts in the practice.

## AIR RIFLES

A number of hunting-quality pellet rifles exist. These are allowed in many states for taking small game. A number of manufacturers such as RWS, Benjamin Sheridan, Crosman, and Daisy make high-powered models in the air gun line that are more than capable of being used for hunting. Be sure that they fire a pellet faster than 700 feet per second (fps) at a minimum before considering using one for hunting. Air rifles that fire at speeds less than that should be used for target practice only.

When using an air rifle for game, be sure that you load it with hunting pellets rather than those meant for targets. The difference is in the shape.

*Never use the scope on your rifle or airgun to scan an area for game. This violates the First Commandment of gun safety—you must only point your rifle at something you intend to destroy. Bring a pair of binoculars to identify legal targets before you raise and aim your firearm.*

Hunting pellets will be pointed like the one pictured at the bottom of page 20, while target pellets will have a flat head. These guns are not toys. A powerful air rifle with pointed pellets such as a .036-gram .177 caliber is capable of taking small game out to 100 feet or more.

Of course, remember that these pellets are much smaller than bullets. With this in mind, shot placement is very important. While you should always try for headshots when hunting small game, headshots are mandatory with an air rifle. Using one of these guns is ideal on very small game such as pest birds like blackbirds, cowbirds, starlings, and sparrows, but do not rule them out for all manner of squirrel and rabbit.

## MUZZLELOADERS

With a crack, a boom, and a cloud of smoke, these firearms are a throwback to the 1800s. Unlike modern firearms that use smokeless powder and one-piece ammunition, these guns use black powder and must be loaded step by step with several components. Typically, they are loaded from the front of the gun, or muzzle, hence their name. First goes the powder, then a patch, and finally the bullet. Then the gun is primed and fired.

The first settlers in the New World used muzzleloaders to harvest game and these types of guns can still work very well for that. Muzzleloading shotguns are very popular in some parts of the country. These throwbacks to the days of Daniel Boone and Davy Crockett can be used on every type of furry or feathered small game. Be sure to check your local regulations. As long as they are approved in your area, these traditional guns can be extremely fun to shoot.

## THINK ABOUT YOUR FEET

If hunting and scouting for game sounds like a lot of walking around, you are right. Unlike deer hunters, who often sit in tree stands and may not move for hours, many small game hunters spend a lot of their time on the move. To keep your feet happy, make sure you wear sturdy but comfortable boots and thick socks.

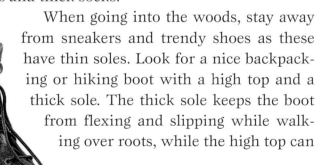

When going into the woods, stay away from sneakers and trendy shoes as these have thin soles. Look for a nice backpacking or hiking boot with a high top and a thick sole. The thick sole keeps the boot from flexing and slipping while walking over roots, while the high top can

*A sturdy pair of waterproof boots are an essential part of every hunter's equipment.*

*Black powder hunting for small game is not closely regulated, and hunters may use their muzzleloading firearms to take any small game that is in season.*

help prevent sprained and strained ankles. Try on several pairs before you make your choice, and then make sure you break them in before heading into the woods.

Keep your feet clean, dry, and your toenails cut straight across to prevent ingrown nails and sores. Watch where you walk on the trail or in the field and choose each step with care. Your feet will thank you for it later.

## STAY DRY

Nothing can ruin a hunting trip like getting wet. While you should check the weather reports before leaving for the woods, you still need to prepare for water. No clothing is completely waterproof, no matter what the tags say, but the smart hunter looks for hats, gloves, and

*If you are going to be hunting in an isolated area far from home, it's a good idea to bring a backpack with some essential gear, just in case you wind up lost or stranded. Some survival items to include are rope (many hunters prefer paracord), snacks or MREs, a compass or small GPS device, flashlight, extra warm clothes and socks, a small saw, toilet paper, a tarp, several Mylar thermal blankets, and matches or matchless fire-starters.*

jackets that are water resistant. An emergency poncho, or even a large trash bag, is an inexpensive item that can be stuffed into a pocket just in case.

Even if it does not rain, there is the possibility of stumbling into ponds or deep puddles. It is a good idea to take an extra pair of socks on the trail with you, so you can change into them if your feet get wet. If you wear wet socks for too long, you can develop painful conditions such as trench foot, which can ruin your hunting experience.

Hypothermia, which is a life threatening condition that can come when cold and wet, is easily preventable. Preventing the loss of body heat when it is colder than 65° Fahrenheit (18° Celsius) is the key. Many veteran hunters use natural hunting items made of wool or treated leathers. They do so because these can still provide warmth even when wet. Materials that are more modern include Gore-Tex and Thinsulate, which do much the same thing.

Remember, dry is warm, wet is cold.

## BE PREPARED

In the woods, things can go wrong quickly. Weather conditions can change, accidents can happen, you can get lost. You can be prepared for problems by checking the weather before you leave, packing a first aid kit, and having a map of your hunting area. Being even more prepared would include learning how to spot changing weather, taking a First Aid/CPR class, and learning how to use a GPS. To add an extra layer to this, consider bringing rain gear and extra clothes, carrying a cellphone, and packing a compass. Check your gear before going on your hunt to make sure you have thought of everything. As the saying goes, "the successful hunter is the one who is prepared."

## Chapter 4

# Tips and Tricks

**H**unting is not a race. The wilderness was there since the dawn of time and there it is full of animals. Never get rushed while hunting. Those who rush, rush, rush, in this sport end up missing out the most. They miss the soothing calm that is the great outdoors. More importantly, running around in the woods can lead to missing out on the animals themselves.

Some trips to the woods never result in finding the game you are looking for. Do not get discouraged. For every hunting trip that washes out, another will happen that works out great. Treasure every step, every minute, and every breath taken in the field. It is those moments—not just taking game—that make a hunting trip successful.

## SCOUT IN ADVANCE

For a hunting trip to have the best chance of success, you must go where the animals are. You need to make decisions about where to hunt before the season starts. Since there are limits on the number of days you can hunt during each season, it's important to do your home-

*Most state game or wildlife commissions maintain online databases on their websites, enabling hunters to search for gamelands that are nearby.*

work ahead of time. Around the country, small game seasons typically open in the fall and run through the spring. Therefore, the smart hunter does his scouting for good hunting areas during the summer months.

If you know of private land where you can hunt, that's great. If not, there are thousands of acres of public land in every state set aside for hunting. Come up with a list of potential hunting areas, and then visit each one. Get out and walk around, looking for animal sign. Know what things draw the type of game you will be after, especially sources of food and water.

Public management areas often have very good trails and roads. A summer scouting trip to these preserves should include a stop at the ranger's station. There you can get maps and more information that can prove very useful in your search for a good spot to hunt.

After you have visited some areas, you can still do additional research on them at home. Go online and check services such as Google Earth to see aerial photos of the area. You want to make sure you're hunting in open woods or fields whenever possible, as more space without people and roads usually means more animals. Getting this type of top-down view can also help you find ponds and streams you may not have noticed during your scouting trip.

Social media like Facebook and Twitter can help in your search for good hunting spots. Each state has numerous social media groups in which sportsmen share information. It costs nothing to become a member of these groups, but the tips you can get from them could lead to a better hunting experience.

## OBEY THE LAW

Each state regulates its own wildlife resources. State wildlife agencies decide what animals can be hunted, how many can be harvested each year, and where and when hunters can take game. The seasons, as well as the equipment and methods that hunters may use, can vary widely from state to state. For instance, some states, such as Alaska, allow hunting small game with legally owned suppressed (silenced) rifles or pistols, while other states do not allow the use of suppressors.

Be sure to check your local laws and make sure that you abide by all the rules of the area. Get your license and follow the limits for what it covers. There will typically be a "bag limit" and "possession limit" for each species in season. A bag limit restricts the size and number of animals that the hunter may kill and keep in a single day. The possession limit is the total number of animals a hunter can keep during a hunting trip. Often, when it comes to small game or waterfowl, the possession limit is two or three times the bag limit. So for example, in Texas the bag limit for ducks is

*A U.S. Fish and Wildlife Service law enforcement officer discusses hunting regulations with a hunter at Sand Lake National Wildlife Refuge in South Dakota.*

six, and the possession limit is three times the bag limit. This means that a hunter could harvest a total of 18 ducks during a hunting trip, shooting no more than 6 per day. Be sure you know the bag and possession limits for the animals that you hunt, and be able to recognize the differences between various species of that animal.

Pay close attention to the requirements for hunter's education (HE) courses. These courses cover not only safety, but survival, local animal species, and emergency first aid. In most states, it is mandatory to take and pass one of these before you can even apply for a hunting license. Be sure to carry your HE card with you when you are hunting.

Be prepared to meet game wardens when practicing your sport. Do not make the mistake of trying to avoid these law enforcement offi-

*Before you go hunting, take time to make sure the sights on your rifle are properly calibrated. This is called "sighting in" your rifle. The best place to do this is at a shooting range, as there will often be some sort of bench rest you can use to provide a steady platform. The steadier your rifle is when it's being sighted, the more accurate it will be. When sighting in your rifle, use the same type of ammunition that you're planning to use when you hunt, because different bullet weights or powder loads will change the trajectory of your shot and could be the difference between a kill and a miss.*

cers, as this will make you appear to be hiding something. When you are approached by a game warden, keep your finger away from the trigger of your rifle and make sure the muzzle is always pointed in a safe direction. Offer to show the game warden your HE card and license, even if they don't ask for it. Answer their questions honestly, even if you accidentally broke a regulation. Honesty is not just a good policy when talking to a game warden, it is the only responsible one.

## PRACTICE BEFORE YOUR TRIP

The last thing you want to do when hunting is fire your rifle or shotgun for the first time. Not only is this unsafe, but you have no guarantee that the gun is even functioning properly. The sights may be off. The gun may have a defect in the way it was made. You may even have bought the wrong ammunition. The best thing for a beginning hunter to do is to get used to his firearm before hitting the woods.

First, read your manual completely with your unloaded gun nearby, so that you can compare illustrations to the firearm. Learn how to work the safety catch and action, as well as how to load it and unload it properly. Once you've familiarized yourself with the gun's operation, take it to a safe range that is designed for shooting the type of firearm you have. For instance, do not take a handgun to a rifle range, or a rifle to a sporting clays stand. Once there, following all the range rules, be sure to get enough target practice in to make sure everything works properly. All guns need to be checked for proper function. Rifles and handguns have sights that need to be adjusted, while shotguns will need to be patterned to see how their shot spreads.

If you'll be hunting with a shotgun, it's a good idea to visit a clays stand. There, you can practice shooting at moving clay targets thrown from projectors. This can really improve your sense of how to properly lead a target with your shotgun.

If you need more help, check with the range to see if they have a certified firearms instructor for referral. Don't feel embarrassed. Keep in mind every instructor you talk with had to be shown what to do at one time as well.

Every minute spent at the range will pay off in the field.

*Chapter 5*

# Hunting Feathered Game

Although there are thousands of species of birds in the United States, only a few types of birds are considered small game and actively hunted. For instance, it is illegal to hunt raptors, such as eagles, hawks, turkey vultures, and owls. These birds of prey are considered "apex predators," and are important for healthy ecosystem functioning. Federal laws protect raptors, and this helps to safeguard other bird species.

Every bird hunter should first be a bird watcher. It is a good idea to read a few bird books with very good illustrations so that you understand the small differences between species. You need to be able to look at the shape of a bird's wing, the size of its tail, its markings, and how it flies and walks to identify it.

Small game birds are harvested almost exclusively with shotguns. In fact, most states require shotguns for bird hunting, banning the use of rifles. One exception is in the case of very small non-game birds, such as sparrows, which can be taken with pellet rifles.

With the above in mind, let us look at some of the most popular game birds.

*The mourning dove has a trim body with a long tail that tapers to a point. It is marked with black spots on the upper wing and a pinkish wash on under-parts. In flight, these birds show white tips on the outer tail feathers.*

## DOVE

Across the country, the late summer begins with dove hunting. These fast and fluttery little birds make difficult targets as they streak across the fields. On the bright side, if you miss the first one, another will surely be along soon, as they usually come in great numbers. This helps even the odds of taking a dove in the hunter's favor.

These birds include the pointed-tailed mourning dove and the white-winged dove.

Doves are part of a group known as non-perching upland game birds. This means you will find them either on the ground or in the sky, not in trees. Corn or grain fields that have been recently harvested are a popular spot for dove hunting, as the birds will flock there to dine on fallen grains. Since doves must consume small rocks to help them digest the seeds and grain that they eat, you can often find them in gravel patches near streams. Before you go dove hunting, take a good pair of binoculars and scout for likely sites a few days in advance.

Once you locate a good dove area, get comfortable and wait. Especially good times for hunting are early morning (before 9 A.M.) and late afternoon (after 3 P.M.). You'll need to blend in to the landscape, so wear camouflage clothing, as doves have good eyesight and won't come near if they spot a hunter. Hide in tall grass or brush, or set up a blind of corn stalks. Doves are not the brightest of birds, and can be tricked into coming closer with the use of battery powered decoys that use spinning wings. Flushing birds from high grass or cooing them in can also have good results.

Be sure to bring several boxes of shotgun shells, typically Number 7 or 8 shot, if going after Mr. Dove. They are small, fast targets, known for flying in anything but a straight line. It's not uncommon for dove hunters to get just three or four birds for every box of shotgun shells they use. Still, at the end of the day, having a nice pile of doves to cook is worth it.

## QUAIL

A close cousin of the dove is the chubby little quail. Bobwhite quail are a favorite of small game hunters in the eastern United States, from Georgia to New York and west to the Mississippi River. In many states, quail season opens in mid-April; however, some states have a fall quail season.

Unlike other game birds, you don't need to wear camouflage when hunting quail. In fact, some states require hunters to wear safety orange during quail season.

Quail prefer to hide in weedy areas where the grass isn't too tall. During the morning, they feed on seeds along the ground, then they

*A male and female pair of northern bobwhite quail sit in a field of purple spring violets. These game birds have rounded bodies, small heads, and short tails. Males have a black-and-white head pattern, while females have a buff-colored throat and eyebrow.*

rest in the weeds during the afternoon. Quail prefer to walk or run on the ground, and have to be flushed into flight most of the time. A trained bird dog can help flush quail, or the hunter can do this himself by simply walking through the field where the birds are located. When flushed, quail typically fly short distances and stay low to the ground. You'll want to use Number 8 shot shells for these game birds. The key to success is finding their feeding and resting areas in advance.

## GROUSE

Popular in northern states, the grouse is a very chicken-like fat bird. They spend their whole lives in the woods, eating flowers and bugs. In different parts of the country, these birds vary in color from grey in the Rocky Mountain States to red on the Pacific coast. Grouse are very afraid of birds of prey such as hawks. To protect themselves from these predators, they will nest in thick branches. These birds are masters of camouflage and will sit very still, just feet away from you.

*The sharp-tailed grouse is found on the American Great Plains, and is sometimes nicknamed the "Prairie Chicken."*

The best way to hunt grouse is with a good bird dog to do the flushing for you. When they finally try to make a getaway, be prepared for a flash of feathers and be ready to shoot fast but safe. Number 8 is the shot shell of choice.

## SNIPE AND RAILS

Along the shorelines of marsh and streams are a whole series of birds that like to hide in the tall grass. These include rails and snipes. Rails are stubby birds that use their long beaks to probe the mudflats and shoreline for food. Snipes are similar but have shorter legs.

*The snipe is a medium-sized shorebird found in wet, grassy spots. It uses its long bill to probe in the mud for food. The snipe's camouflage is so good that these birds are often not seen before they are flushed from the grass.*

While these two species are often found together, they couldn't be more different when spooked. The rail will hop into the air, fly a short distance, and then land again nearby. The snipe will take off and fly amazing zigzag patterns. These little daredevils are so hard to hit that the word "sniper," referring to a military marksman, originated in the 18th century as a term to describe someone capable of shooting one of these challenging game birds.

Because these birds live in wet, marshy areas, a good pair of waterproof rubber boots is essential. Hip boots or even breathable waders also work well. For this type of hunting, you may also want to use a canoe or shallow-draft boat to get to where the birds are. Number 7 or 8 shot will work well when hunting snipe and rails.

Keep in mind, when hunting birds that live in wetlands, you're required to use non-toxic shot. The U.S. Fish and Wildlife Service outlawed the use of lead shot for hunting waterfowl in 1991, and the restrictions were later expanded to include hunting for wading birds like snipe, rails, moorhens, and the like. This was done to alleviate lead poisoning among birds that accidentally ingested shot pellets that had fallen to the bottoms of lakes or ponds. Non-toxic shot may be required in some upland areas as well, so be aware of the restrictions before you set out on your hunting trip. Steel shot and other non-toxic varieties have slightly different ballistics than lead shot, so always practice with the same type of shells you plan to take into the field.

## MOORHENS, GALLINULES, AND COOTS

These migratory game birds can often be found in areas where there are ducks. They aren't ducks, however; they're actually related to rails. Moorhens, gallinules, and coots don't have webbed feet, don't fly in flocks, and don't respond to decoys or calls. They are commonly called "marsh hens" or "mudhens," and as these names suggest they gather around marshy areas where there is lots of standing water.

Moorhens and gallinules are very placid and are not easily spooked. When found, they are likely to run across floating lily pads in the marsh. They rarely fly, and when they do will travel only a short distance before trying to hide. These birds are not legal to hunt in all states, but they are a popular small game species in the Southeast. It is easier to hunt them from shallow-draft boats; polling the boat through marsh grasses and cattails tends to flush moorhens

*A common moorhen stands between a pair of teal ducks.*

*Coots are often mistaken for ducks, as they are found in ponds and waterways throughout the United States. However, these water birds are more closely related to rails and cranes than to ducks. Coots have dark bodies and white faces.*

from their habitat. Some hunters will combine moorhen hunting with scouting in preparation for the duck season that in many states follows a few weeks later.

Coots can be found in great numbers in swampy areas of the country from coast to coast. In Louisiana they are known as *pouldeau*, which is a French word that means "water hen." This name is entirely correct as these birds walk around the shoreline like chickens pecking at food. Without webbed feet, they have to run for longer distances to get their stubby bodies into the air. Most states have generous bag limits on coots because they are so numerous. It is relatively easy to "limit out" on these birds, as they will float up to hunters in large groups, and even when scattered coots will reform in a few minutes just a short distance away. Number 7-1/2 or 8 size steel shot works fine for migratory game birds.

## PHEASANT

The ring-necked pheasant is a common game bird found throughout the United States. This long-tailed bird is one of the larger game birds taken by small game hunters. Adult males can have a wingspread up to three feet, although typically these birds are about the size of large chickens. To bring down this larger game bird, you'll need to use heavier shot, such as Number 4 or 6. Pheasants are capable of taking smaller shot pellets and still flying away.

*Male ring-necked pheasants like this one are brightly colored, with red faces, copper and gold plumage, and a white collar. Females are brown and tend to blend into the fields where they live.*

Pheasants were originally brought to the U.S. from Europe as game birds during the 19th century. Today, these birds have become widespread, especially in grain-producing areas of the Midwest as well as the northeastern states. For example, in 2012 hunters in South Dakota, where pheasants are the state bird, bagged more than 1.2 million pheasants.

Pheasants prefer grassy fields and farmed areas, where they can eat wild grains as well as wheat crops at harvest time. With that in mind, be prepared for a lot of walking through high grass during pheasant season. These birds are fast on their feet and normally run first before flying. Pheasants will often return to the same area day after day when flushed away, so back-to-back hunting on the same field over a week can bring good results. The smart hunter scouts to learn pheasants' escape patterns each day, and is waiting for them.

## WOODCOCK

These migratory birds are active at night, flying from Canada down to Mexico and back each year. During the day, they camp out in scrub near sources of water. In different parts of the country, they are called mudsnipe or bogsuckers because of this. They primarily eat earthworms with their long beaks, so if you find areas where the earth is open without a lot of grass, with scrub and water nearby, odds are good that woodcock are there during the season. Flushing in this scrub will send these little guys skyward.

This little robin-sized bird flies like an acrobat, even more so than the dove. Unlike the dove, they do not come in great numbers. Therefore, this bird is hunted for challenge, rather than meat. If you find dove too easy, try woodcock.

## DUCKS AND GEESE

Among small game birds, waterfowl are considered the top of the line. These birds include all sorts of ducks, merganser, and geese. Waterfowl were almost hunted into extinction by the early 20th century, but their populations have enjoyed a comeback. This is due to the fact that waterfowl are among the most protected game in the country. To go after these birds, you will have to buy both state and federal duck stamps. Some states also make hunters buy special waterfowl licenses as well. You also must use non-toxic shot when hunting waterfowl, to keep from polluting their habitat with lead. Despite all of the regulations, these birds make some of the prettiest trophies and best table fare.

Waterfowl can spot something that is out of the ordinary while they are flying, and they won't come near if they sense danger. For duck or goose hunters, this means camouflage is an important part of strategy. Skilled waterfowl hunters will build blinds within which they can hide. In addition, a skilled hunter can decoy ducks and geese in closer with the right call.

Because steel, tungsten, and other non-toxic shot have different ballis-

*A blind may be an important element of your strategy when hunting ducks or geese.*

*A variety of decoys and calls are available to help you hunt waterfowl like ducks.*

tic properties than lead, the type of shot you choose will affect the shot size. If you're using steel shot, use BBB or BB size for geese and Number 1, 2 or 3 shot for ducks. If you're using tungsten shot, BB or Number 2 will work for geese and Number 2, 4, or 5 shot will work for ducks. Remember, patterning your shotgun with the shot you plan to use before you go hunting will make it more likely that you'll bring home ducks or geese.

Limits on waterfowl can be very tricky. For instance in Mississippi in 2013 you could get, "4 mallards, 1 mottled duck, 3 wood ducks, 2 redheads, 4 scaup, 1 canvasback, and 2 pintail" per day. Thus you can see why it is extremely important to be able to tell different types of waterfowl apart. You have to be able to look at a flock flying overhead and know whether they are loosely regulated Snow Geese, or strictly regulated Canadian Geese. The first few times you go hunting waterfowl, it's a good idea to go with a more experienced duck hunter or hire a guide to show you the ropes.

## CROWS AND PEST BIRDS

Crows are a non-game pest bird, meaning they are typically not shot for food, but rather for sport. Crows have been called "bandit birds" for generations and are responsible for killing thousands of other birds and baby animals each year. They also hurt crops and plants and carry diseases such as West Nile and chronic wasting diseases, which can destroy deer herds. Hunters help keep the crow population in check.

The best way to hunt crows is by using decoys and calls. Camouflage is very important, as these birds are sight hunters and can spot an undisguised hunter from a distance. They come in low and slow, making for easy shots with Number 7 or 8 shot.

Along with the crow and grackle, many states also list a number of so-called pest birds that can be harvested year-round (open season). These typically include sparrows, starlings, and pigeons. Because they birds are non-migratory, they usually do not have as many restrictions as crows. However, always check your local wildlife laws before heading into the woods with your shotgun.

*A trained dog can help to flush game like this ring-necked pheasant.*

## MAN'S BEST FRIEND

Many a small game hunter will have a dog as a partner. In bird seasons, good field dogs like pointers and spaniels will help you flush birds. Others, like Labradors and Golden Retrievers, can be trained to fetch harvested game from the field. Dogs can be bought already trained, but there is a lot to be learned if you want to train your own. Remember to be patient and look after the dog's needs while in the field as well as your own.

If you do not have a trained dog to flush game birds, you can usually get good results with two or more hunters walking slowly through the field about 10 yards (9m) apart. Be careful to not get ahead or behind each other and always have the barrel of your shotgun pointed in a safe direction when hunting as a team. You may want to practice this in the summer with your hunting buddies, without loaded guns.

Chapter 6

# Hunting Furred Game

In addition to the wide variety of game birds, small game hunters also enjoy a range of options when it comes to hunting animals that travel on four legs. These include squirrels, rabbits, raccoons, and opossums, along with predators such as coyote and bobcat, and feral hogs. Let us look at these.

### SQUIRREL

These bushy-tailed tree dwellers are some of the most common animals in the woods. Odds are if you have two trees, you will find a squirrel in one of them. Their numbers are high and in many states they are the most popular small game animal. For instance, in Louisiana more than 900,000 squirrels are harvested every year.

Look for a good thick population of these critters before the season. Once they are in season, it's best to walk into that location before dawn, sit quietly against a tree, and listen. Be silent. Be still. After legal hunting hours start, watch for a squirrel and carefully take your shot. As long as you are camouflaged, you can usually take two or three squirrels before the rest start hiding. Typically, they will start moving again within a few minutes, so just wait them out.

Another good method of squirrel hunting is the stalk. Simply take a few steps with your gun pointed in a safe direction and your finger off the trigger. Then stop, listen, watch, and wait. If you do not find anything, repeat this until you come across those tree crawlers. When you spot a squirrel, slowly and deliberately bring your rifle into firing position and wait for a clear shot.

Small caliber rifles such as .22s work best when hunting squirrels. Be sure to aim for the head or high shoulder area, and try to make sure that the bushy tail is in front of a good thick tree limb so the bullet will be stopped behind it. If you'd rather hunt with a shotgun, use Number 5 or 6 shot. However, with a shotgun remember that you won't be as accurate at a longer distance, and you will have to pull out numerous pellets if you plan to eat your harvest.

Be extremely careful during squirrel season, as in many states it overlaps deer season. That blur of movement in the treetop 50 feet away may be a camouflaged deer hunter in a tree stand. Always be sure you've got a squirrel in your sights before pulling the trigger.

## RABBITS AND HARES

No one ever said that rabbits are smart. One of the reasons they can reproduce in such great numbers is to make up for this fact of life.

*Stalking is the slow, silent pursuit of an animal, done until the hunter is close enough for a clear shot at his target. This is an effective way to hunt small game animals.*

They gather in almost any wooded area that has lots of thick natural grasses and wide leaf weeds. This is their food source. A good way to scout for flop ears is to go before the season to these places right at dawn and dusk, watching for bunnies.

Once the season opens up, hunting for rabbits can be as simple as taking a walk through the area you've scouted. Take about ten steps, wait and watch, then repeat. Eventually a rabbit will dart away, flushed from his hiding spot. You have to be a fast shot, though, as they will scamper away faster than just about any other animal.

If you miss the rabbit, remember that spot, as they usually will circle back to it. Shotguns of any gauge with Number 5 or 6 shot will do the trick on all but the biggest woodland rabbits. If you are hunting large desert jackrabbits in places like Arizona and California, small caliber rifles are preferred.

## RACCOON

These large nocturnal scavengers used to be extremely popular game animals for their fur. However, in the past few decades this has fallen out of favor. While they are not as hunted today as they once were, there are still large groups of sportsmen that love raccoon hunts. Raccoons will eat almost anything, and often raid garbage cans late at night.

While often hunted in the southeast with the help of "coon dogs" like hounds and beagles, you can also hunt these critters on your own. This often involves night hunting with strong portable LED lights (check your state regulations regarding them) or the use of calls during daytime to bring them in. Shotguns using Number 4, 5, or 6 shot, or .22 rifles are the most popular choices for harvesting these animals.

*Raccoons typically live in wooded areas and forage for food near bodies of water.*

## VERMIN

Every state has a list of four-legged small animals that are considered nuisance vermin. While each state is different, this list often includes armadillos, chipmunk, groundhogs, moles, opossums, skunk, beaver, and various types of rats. Few states have actual seasons on these

*For hunting rats and other small vermin, .22 cartridges loaded with shot, rather than a bullet, can be used. The pellets are typically #12 shot, which is much smaller than the shot used for hunting birds. The blue plastic holding the shot in place shatters when the gun is fired, allowing it to spread like shot from a shotgun.*

pests—for the most part, it is legal to harvest them at any time—but always be sure you check the rules for your state before you hunt.

Not many hunters specialize in harvesting these animals, as they are not typically used for food. However, hunters do make worthwhile contributions to the environment by taking these pests. For instance, beavers and nutria rats are well known contributors to flooding problems in the Southeast, while armadillos are believed to carry diseases that can affect human populations.

## PREDATORS

In the United States, there have always been predators in the mountains and forests. Over the past several centuries, the numbers of large predators such as wolves and bears have been greatly reduced. Nevertheless, good numbers of small predators such as bobcat, fox, and coyote remain. The regulations on these last three vary widely from state to state, but in most places, all are on the approved list for small game hunters.

As a rule, these predators stay in their dens during daylight hours and are usually just seen at dawn and dusk. They prey on smaller animals. In most areas, they are at or near the top of the food chain, and therefore fear no predators other than the hunter. Here again, the conservationist hunter must step in to control overpopulation.

The best technique for taking smaller predators is to stand hunt, and use calling devices to attract them to your location. These devices

*Coyotes are active in the early morning and at night. When you hear them howling, take note of the location and ask the property owner if you can hunt on their land. Most farmers and ranchers will be more than happy to let you remove these predators from their properties. When hunting, make sure the wind is in your face. Coyotes have a keen sense of smell, and will avoid hunters they detect.*

mimic the cries of their prey, such as injured rabbits. A smart hunter targeting predator animals must be very careful about camouflage, including scent control. Typically, most hunters prefer to use small-caliber centerfire rifles chambered for such flat-shooting rounds as .223 or .25-06. However, rifles chambered for .22 magnum rounds can be effective. Shotguns loaded with #2, #3, or #4 shot can also be used to hunt vermin, although keep in mind that these firearms will have a much shorter range.

## WILD HOGS

When explorers such as Hernando de Soto arrived in North America during the 16th century, they brought herds of pigs with them, intending to use them as food. Over time, as the explorers traveled into North America, some of these swine escaped into the wilderness. Today, their decedents have spread throughout much of the continent, and the feral hog population numbers in the millions. Wild hogs are an invasive species; they damage crops and property and push out native animal species.

Wild hogs are considered nuisance animals, rather than small game, and in many places hunters are permitted to harvest them all year round (open season). In states with very large populations of wild hogs, such as those in the southeast, there are few restrictions on how they can be harvested. For instance, in Texas and Florida wild hogs can be taken through night hunts, trapping, and other means that are normally prohibited.

These animals can be very dangerous. Adults can have razor sharp tusks that can seriously injure hunters. Their thick hide requires that they be taken with larger caliber rifles, such as those chambered for .243 Winchester, .30-30, or a similar round. Shotguns loaded with slugs or buckshot can also be effective. When shooting at a wild hog, aim for the lower shoulder area, as that's where the vital organs are located.

Feral swine meat is very good to eat. As with any game, proper field dressing and thorough cooking are always recommended. Swine meat must be cooked to 165° Fahrenheit to kill disease organisms and parasites.

*In many southern and southeastern states, wild hogs can typically be hunted year-round and there are no bag or possession limits. This makes hunting these creatures a great opportunity for hunters to practice their skills and spend time in the field when other game seasons are closed.*

## Chapter 7

# After the Hunt

The hunt is not over after the gun goes off and the target drops. There is still much to do: cleaning and preparing the animal, and reporting the harvest. Then comes the fun stuff: cooking your game, and recapping the experience with your hunting buddies.

### CLEANING

If you have never hunted before, this most likely will be your first experience with meat that did not come from the store. As soon as the animal drops, its meat is fresh, but it will begin spoiling with every passing minute. The meat must be quickly cooled, and kept cool until it can be cleaned and refrigerated. The best way to do this is to have a cooler filled with ice on hand that you can put your harvest in as soon as possible. While "still hunting," such as for doves, the cooler can also double as a chair.

As soon as possible, remove the entrails and organs of the animal from the meat, as they start to spoil first. If you are too late, the flesh will feel slimy and have a bad smell. Never eat wild game that you are not 100 percent certain is still fresh.

*A sharp knife with a gut hook is a useful tool for cleaning small game in the field. Start by using the knife blade to make a long but shallow cut in the belly of the bird or creature. Be careful—if you cut too deeply, you will puncture the entrails, and that will cause the meat to spoil. Use the gut hook to "unzip" the game, revealing the entrails. In a small animal like a rabbit, these are connected at the throat and anus, so cutting those two points will allow you to remove them all together. On a larger game bird like a pheasant, insert the gut hook in the anus or throat and twist it a few times. When you withdraw the gut hook, most of the entrails will be entwined on the hook and removed. You may have to do this a few times to make sure everything has been removed.*

Once it has been cleaned, you can soak the meat in ice water or milk to remove any blood or gamey taste. Carefully examine the meat for shotgun pellets and bullet fragments, and then be sure to remove them. Lead pellets can be poisonous if ingested, and you could break a tooth if you bite down on a pellet while eating.

Removing feathers can be done more easily if you dunk the bird in a pot of scalding hot (not boiling) water several times. Heat the water to about 150°F (66°C), hold the bird by the feet, and dip it into the pot for 20 to 30 seconds. Do this two or three times, then hang the bird from a string by the leg and pull out the feathers. Be meticulous—some areas, such as the wings, have tiny feathers that are hard to remove. An alternative to plucking is to simply skin the bird, taking all of the feathers with it.

Keep in mind that an animal's diet will affect the overall taste of its meat.

*These two pheasants have been plucked and are ready to cook.*

For instance, animals like squirrel that eat hard nuts and bitter acorns will be the "gamiest," while birds like doves that eat seed and grain will taste lighter. Removing the entrails promptly, and without accidentally cutting into the stomach, intestines, or bowels, will help to minimize the gamy flavor of the meat.

It's appropriate to keep your small game harvest out of sight of the public until you make it back home. This is done out of respect for people who may not agree with hunting or become queasy at the sight of dead animals.

## RECIPES

A quick search of the Internet can provide any number of recipes for wild game. Here are a couple of our favorites.

### BACON SAUTÉED SQUIRREL

Ingredients
 1 squirrel, cleaned and deboned
 1/4 cup flour
 dash of salt and pepper
 5 or 6 strips of bacon, diced
 1 tablespoon of garlic, minced
 2 cups of chicken broth
 1 cup of fresh mushrooms

Directions
Take your clean squirrel meat and coat it with the seasonings and flour. Set to the side. Cook bacon in a deep skillet and remove, leaving the grease. Add your floured squirrel to the bacon grease and cook until the meat is browned. While this is cooking, warm the chicken broth in a separate pot. When the squirrel meat has browned, pour in the warm broth, add the garlic, bacon, and mushrooms, then bring the mixture to a simmer. Cover the skillet tightly and cook on low for about an hour. This makes a feast for one or a great meal for two with rice or potatoes and a vegetable added.

## Game Bird Bake

Ingredients

    Several small bird breasts (dove, quail, etc.)
    1/4 cup of flour
    salt and pepper, other spices to taste
    6 tablespoons of butter
    2 cups of chicken broth
    1 small onion, finely diced

Directions

You can marinate the breasts overnight in milk in the refrigerator; this will make them taste milder and less gamey, but it's not required. Dust the breasts with flour and seasoning, then set them to the side. Melt 4 tablespoons of butter in a skillet, then place the breasts into the skillet and brown them on both sides. Place browned breasts in a casserole or baking pan and set them to the side. Keeping the bird drippings in the skillet, melt 2 more tablespoons of butter and then sauté the finely cut onion until it is soft. Then slowly add the chicken broth. Once this has been mixed and heated, pour the mixture over the breasts in the casserole pan. Preheat the oven to 325°F (163°C). Bake covered for one hour, then serve. You can adjust this recipe as needed; plan to prepare two breasts for each dinner guest.

## DOCUMENTING

It is the duty of a hunter to report their harvest. If you harvested any migratory birds like doves or duck, you have to complete the Federal HIP survey. For hunters on public land, it is always smart, even if it is not required, to stop in at the ranger station and report how your day went. Some states require that the hunter call and make a report, while others will mail surveys to your home at the end of the season.

You can get more information on your state's requirements when you get your license. Remember to make these reports as it helps in conservation. The information you give will be added to that collected from thousands of other hunters to get the big picture.

*If you've been issued a license to hunt migratory birds, you must file a report on your harvest—even if you did not bag anything. In most states, reports can be submitted electronically through the internet, or mailed to the state game commission.*

## MEMORIES

Take pictures of your harvest and keep a hunter's journal. Or better yet, start your own internet journal on www.forever.com. This will prove invaluable to you as keepsakes as you get older. It will also help keep your memory fresh for coming years as to what worked, where the game was, and what did not work. As the years pass, you will move from being a beginning hunter to an expert one. These words and images can help pass on your gained wisdom for generations to come.

Someone else has taken before every step you will take in the field. Those who follow will take every step you take in the future. Respect yourself, respect the animals, and respect the sport.

Good luck out there.

# Glossary

**animal sign**—traces that animals leave behind, like scat (feces), tracks, down, or food remnants that show they have been there.

**bag limit**—the number, established by state or federal wildlife agencies, of a particular type of animal that can be harvested in a day during the hunting season.

**camouflage**—the art of blending into the surroundings so that a hunter is concealed from the game being stalked. Camouflage is accomplished by imitating the colors and textures of the environment, or by using natural elements such as branches, grass, or cornstalks as cover.

**centerfire**—a cartridge in which the primer or primer assembly is seated in a pocket or recess in the center of the base of the brass casing; this term also refers to a firearm that uses centerfire cartridges. All modern shotguns and most handguns and rifles use centerfire cartridges.

**feral**—an animal that has escaped domestication and become wild.

**flush**—to frighten game that is hiding out into the open. Flushing can be done by hunters walking through brush or by trained dogs.

**gauge**—a unit of measurement used to express the bore diameter of a shotgun's barrel. The gauge is determined by the weight of a metal ball that fits in the firearm. For example, a ball that is one-twelfth of a pound would fit in a 12 gauge shotgun; a slightly larger ball that is one-tenth of a pound would fit in a 10 gauge shotgun.

**HE card**—a Hunter's Education card issued by the state. Typically, a hunter will need this in order to get a hunting license, and it should be carried with the hunter at all times.

**hunter's orange**—also called blaze orange, safety orange, or international orange, this bright color is worn for safety in the woods.

**invasive species**—an animal that is not native to the area, but has been introduced. These animals can harm the environment because native animals or plants are not able to cope with them.

**magazine**—a device that holds multiple ammunition cartridges under spring pressure, so they can be rapidly loaded into a firearm's chamber.

**mast**—a food source of nuts produced by hardwood trees, such as oak acorns.

**Migratory Bird Harvest Information Program (HIP)**—a program managed by the federal government that collects data on various bird species harvested by hunters.

**muzzle**—the forward end of the barrel where the projectile exits.

**muzzle discipline**—the practice of keeping a firearm's muzzle from pointing at anything that you do not want to destroy.

**negligent discharge**—the accidental firing of a bullet from a gun. This can usually be avoided by observing the rules of firearm safety.

**open season**—a period when restrictions on the hunting of certain types of wildlife are lifted.

**Pittman-Robertson Act**—a federal law that taxes gun and ammunition sales and uses those funds for conservation and hunters' safety education programs.

**poaching**—taking game without the proper license in season, outside of the legal season, or by the use of prohibited techniques (such as spotting or night hunting). Poaching is a crime.

**possession limit**—the maximum amount of game you can have in your control during a multi-day hunting trip. For big-game animals, the possession limit is typically the same as the bag limit. For small game, the possession limit may be two or three times the bag limit.

**ricochet**—the action of a bullet that hits a hard surface and bounces away, usually in a different direction.

**rimfire**—a type of cartridge in which the primer is contained inside the hollow rim of the case. The primer is detonated by the firing pin striking the outside edge of the rim, crushing the rim against the rear face of the barrel. This term also refers to a firearm that uses rimfire cartridges, such as a .17 or .22 caliber rifle.

**scent control**—ensuring that you are not wearing excessive human scents when hunting such as deodorants, perfumes, and scented soaps. Many animals can smell a hunter long before they can see one.

**shot size**—the size of the pellets inside a shotgun shell. Smaller pellets are used for birds and the smallest game; larger pellets are needed for larger game. Shot pellets range in size from Number 12 (the smallest, at one-twentieth of an inch in diameter) to 000 buck (the largest, at more than one-third of an inch in diameter).

**sight radius**—the length from the front sight to the rear sight on a firearm's barrel. The longer this distance, the more accurate the firearm tends to be.

**stalking**—moving through the field or woods slowly and with purpose looking for game. Generally done by slowly walking a few steps, then pausing to look and listen for game, then walking again a few moments later.

**still hunting**—when a hunter sits or stands and waits in an area for a long period, waiting for animals to come to them. Also called posting or stand hunting.

**trigger discipline**—keeping your finger out of the trigger guard and off the trigger until you are lined up on a target and ready to fire.

# Further Reading

Bezzant, John. *Butchering Small Game and Birds: Rabbits, Hares, Poultry and Wild Birds*. Wiltshire, UK: Crowood Press, 2013.

Bowles, Dennis. *From the Tree to the Table. Squirrel Hunting HQ*. Mount Pleasant, S.C.: DBo Enterprises, 2013.

Bussard, Michael E. *NRA Firearms Sourcebook: Your Ultimate Guide to Guns, Ballistics, and Shooting*. Fairfax, Va.: National Rifle Association, 2006.

Dunn, Jon L., and Jonathan Alderfer. *National Geographic Field Guide to the Birds of North America*. Washington, D.C.: National Geographic, 2011.

Fisher, David. *Rabbit Hunting: Secrets of a Master Cottontail Hunter*. New York: Skyhorse Publishing, 2013.

Hasheider, Phillip. *The Complete Book of Butchering, Smoking, Curing, and Sausage Making: How to Harvest Your Livestock & Wild Game*. Minneapolis: Voyageur Press, 2010.

Lawrence, H. Lea. *The Ultimate Guide to Small Game and Varmint Hunting: How to Hunt Squirrels, Rabbits, Hares, Woodchucks, Coyotes, Foxes and More*. Guilford, Conn.: Lyons Press, 2002.

Nickens, T. Edward. *The Field and Stream Total Outdoorsman Manual: 374 Skills YOU Need*. New York: Simon and Schuster, 2011.

Rost, Amy, editor. *Survival Wisdom & Know How: Everything You Need to Know to Thrive in the Wilderness*. New York: Black Dog & Leventhal Publishers, 2007.

# Internet Resources

**http://www.ducks.org**

Ducks Unlimited is dedicated to conservation of wetlands and waterfowl. The organization's website includes articles, waterfowl information, and news of conservation events.

**http://ihea-usa.org/hunting-and-shooting/hunter-education**

The International Hunters Education Association's maintains this website, which offers visitors the opportunity to search for hunter's education courses in their area.

**http://www.nssf.org/safety**

The National Shooting Sports Foundation's web page on firearms safety includes educational videos and articles about safe and responsible gun ownership.

**http://magazine-directory.com/Outdoor-Life.htm**

Website of the magazine *Outdoor Life* includes articles and blog posts on hunting, fishing, and other outdoor activities.

**http://birds.audubon.org/birdid**

The National Audubon Society's online guide to North American birds includes information on many bird species.

**http://www.crowbusters.com**

Crowbusters is a website for crow hunters, which includes articles and tips for those who wish to harvest these pest birds.

**http://www.forever.com**

Newly launched Web site where you can create your own journal with words and images to be shared with future generations.

**http://www.fws.gov/offices/statelinks.html**

At this site, the U.S. Fish and Wildlife Service maintains a directory of all state and territorial fish and wildlife offices across the country.

**http://digitalmedia.fws.gov**

The U.S. Fish and Wildlife Service's digital library includes thousands of wildlife pictures, videos, and maps.

**http://www.boone-crockett.org**

Boone and Crockett Club is an organization that promotes wildlife conservation and hunter safety. It was founded by Theodore Roosevelt in 1887, making it the oldest such organization in the United States.

**http://www.nraila.org/gun-laws/state-laws.aspx**

At this site, the National Rifle Association maintains a state-by-state listing of gun laws related to firearms ownership.

**http://www.odcmp.com**

The Civilian Marksmanship Program (CMP) is a government organization dedicated to training and educating Americans, particularly youths, about the responsible use of firearms.

**http://www.nrainstructors.org/searchcourse.aspx**

This searchable database enables you to find a certified NRA shooting and safety instructor in your local area.

Publisher's Note: The websites listed on this page were active at the time of publication. The publisher is not responsible for websites that have changed their address or discontinued operation since the date of publication. The publisher reviews and updates the websites each time the book is reprinted.

# Index

air rifles (pellet rifles), 20–21, 33

ammunition, 15–16

  air rifle, 20–21

  for bird hunting, 35, 36, 37, 39, 41–42

  for furred game, 46, 47, *48*, 49, 50

  lead shot, *19*, 37–38

  shotgun, 18, 19–20

Bacon Sautéed Squirrel (recipe), 53

bag limits, 29–30, 39

  *See also* limits

binoculars, *21*, 34

birds, 21, 33–34, 54

  and hunting colors, 13

  survey of, 7

  types of, 34–43

blinds, waterfowl, 41

bobwhite quail, 35

bogsuckers. *See* woodcocks

calling devices, 48–49

cleaning animals, 51–54

clothing, hunting, 24–25, 34

conservation, 6–7, 15–16, 48, 54

"coon dogs," 47

  *See also* dogs, hunting

coots, 38, 39

coyote, 48, *49*

crows, 42–43

dogs, hunting, 36, 43, 47

doves, 34–35

ducks, *7*, 13, 41

equipment, 12, 14, 48–49, 51, *52*

  binoculars, *21*, 34

  clothing, 24–25, 34

  footwear, 22, 24, 37

  guns and ammunition, 15–21, *30*

  thermal blankets, 14, *24*

eye and ear protection, 12

feathered game. *See* birds

feral hogs, 49–50

footwear, 22, 24, 37

furred game, 45–50

gallinules, 38

Game Bird Bake (recipe), 54

game wardens, 13, 30–31

geese, 41, 42

grackle, 43

grouse, 36

gun safety, 9–12, *21*

handguns, 20, 31

Harvest Information Program (HIP), 7, 54

Henry, 17

hogs, wild, 49–50

H&R, 17

"hunter orange," 12–13

hunter's education (HE) courses, 30, 31

hunting

  challenges of, 5–6

  and "cleaning" animals, 51–54

  and conservation, 6–7, 15–16, 48, 54

  and documentation, 54

  and equipment, 12, 14, 15–22, 24–25, *30*, 34, 37, 48–49, 51, 52

  and gun safety, 9–12, *21*

  history of, 5

  and a "hunting plan," 13

  laws and regulations, 29–31, 33, 39, 42, 43, 47

  licenses, 29, 30, 31, 41, *55*

  and memories, 55

  safety of, 9, 11–14, 25, 31

  and scouting, 27–29, 34, 40

  as sport, 6

  and stalking, *46*

  *See also* birds; furred game

hunting laws. *See* laws and regulations, hunting

hypothermia, 25

jackrabbits, 47

laws and regulations, hunting, 29–31, 33, 47

  and limits, 29–30, 39, 42, 43

lead shot, *19*, 37–38

  *See also* ammunition

licenses, hunting, 29, 30, 31, 41, *55*

Numbers in ***bold italic*** refer to captions.

limits, 29–30, 39, 42, 43
    *See also* laws and regula-
        tions, hunting

magnum rounds, 16
    *See also* ammunition
Marlin, 17
merganser, 41
migratory birds survey. *See*
    birds
moorhens, 38–39
mourning doves, 34
mudsnipe. *See* woodcocks
muzzleloaders, 22, *23*

National Shooting Sports
    Foundation, 9

pellet rifles (air rifles), 20–21,
    33
pest birds, 43
pheasants, *7*, 39–40
pigeons, 43
Pittman-Robertson Act, 6–7
possession limits, 29–30
    *See also* limits
pouldeau. *See* coots
predators, 7, 48–49

quail, 35–36

rabbits, *7*, 46–47

raccoons, 47
rails, 36–37
ranger's stations, 28, 54
raptors, 33
    *See also* birds
recipes, 53–54
Remington, 17, 19
rifles, 15–16, 31, 46, 49, 50
    action, 17–18
    "sighting," *30*
    types of, 16–18, 20–21, 33
    *See also* shotguns
ring-necked pheasant, 39, *40*,
    *43*
Rossi, 17
Ruger, 17

safety, gun, 9–12
safety colors, 12–13
Savage, 17
scouting, 27–29, 34, 40
    *See also* hunting
seasons, small game, 28, 29, 35,
    46, 48
sharp-tailed grouse, *36*
shells. *See* ammunition
shooting ranges, 31
shot, non-toxic, *19*, 37–38,
    41–42
    *See also* ammunition
shotguns, 31, 46, 49, 50
    action, 19

and bird hunting, 33, 35
    bore sizes, 18, 19–20
    and furred game, 46, 49, 50
    types of, 18, 19
    *See also* rifles
"skylined" targets, *10*
small caliber rounds, 15–16
    *See also* ammunition
small game, 13
    seasons for, 28, 29, 35, 46,
        48
    types of, 5, *7*, 15
    *See also* birds; furred game
snipes, 36–37
sparrows, 43
squirrels, 45–46, 53
stalking, *46*
stamps, duck, 41
starlings, 43
"Survival Rule of Threes," 14

U.S. Fish and Wildlife Service,
    *29*, 37

vermin, 48

waterfowl, 37, 41–42
white-winged dove, 34
wildlife commissions (agen-
    cies), *28*, 29
Winchester, 17
woodcocks, 40–41

# About the Author

Christopher Eger is a writer and trainer with years of experience as a firearms instructor. In his daytime job, he trains for a Department of Homeland Security contractor. When not consumed with that he teaches hunter's safety and writes for numerous websites and shooting magazines with a number of articles and books in print. He started hunting small game at age six.